CALAMITY JANE

CALAMITY JANE

Published by Creative Education, 123 South Broad Street, Mankato, Minnesota 56001
Creative Education is an imprint of The Creative Company
Design and Production by EvansDay Design

Photographs by Buffalo Bill Historical Center; Cody, Wyoming (Vincent Mercaldo Collection *P.71.1612*, cover, p. 2; *P.69.1276*, p. 12), Corbis (Craig Aurness, Bettmann, Jonathan Blair, CORBIS SYGMA, Gerald French, George H. H. Huey, Lake County Museum, Danny Lehman, David Muench, Arthur Rothstein), Kansas State Historical Society

Library of Congress Cataloging-in-Publication Data
Gilbert, Sara. Calamity Jane / by Sara Gilbert.
p. cm. — (Legends of the West)
Includes bibliographical references.
ISBN 1-58341-337-5

1. Calamity Jane, 1852-1903—Juvenile literature. 2. Women pioneers—West (U.S.)—Biography—Juvenile literature. 3. Pioneers—West (U.S.)—Biography—Juvenile literature. 4. West (U.S.)—Biography—Juvenile literature. I. Title. II. Legends of the West (Mankato, Minn.)
F594.C2G65 2005   978.02'092—dc22   2004056168 [B]

First edition

2 4 6 8 9 7 5 3 1

Cover and page 2 photograph:
Calamity Jane, wearing a rare dress instead of her famous buckskin getup

⊰⟞⟞═ **Sara Gilbert** ═⟝⟝⊱

CALAMITY JANE
MAY HAVE ONE OF THE MOST FITTING NICKNAMES EVER.

The life of **Martha Jane Cannary**, who became known as one of the wildest women in the Old West, was a series of treacherous and often troubling adventures. From traveling as a young girl with her family on a five-month journey to Montana to her stint as a scout for General George Armstrong Custer to her daring days in Deadwood, South Dakota, Calamity Jane earned her name the hard way.

Exactly how she earned it, however, is unclear, as are several other stories about her life. But it is a fact that she lived in a time of great change in the United States. During the 1870s and 1880s, many families moved west in hopes of finding better lives. What the majority of them found, as Calamity Jane did, was a dangerous, lawless land.

Calamity Jane was certainly a larger-than-life figure in those early days of the West. Her outrageous behavior was well-documented throughout the years. Whether all of the heroics and harrowing experiences were truth or tall tales, they helped shape the image of the West and of one of its leading ladies, Calamity Jane.

CHAPTER ONE

The Road West

MARTHA JANE CANNARY

WAS BORN, ACCORDING TO HER AUTOBIOGRAPHY,

on May 1, 1852, in Princeton, Missouri,

THE FIRST OF SIX CHILDREN TO

Robert and Charlotte Cannary.

❋ ❋ ❋ ❋

She was a big girl, tall and strong, and she had a head full
of bright red hair. Instead of playing with dolls or helping
with the housework like other girls, Marthy, as she was
known to her family, preferred to seek adventure outdoors.

If there were any schools near her Missouri home, it is unlikely that Marthy attended them. She received little or no formal education, choosing instead to focus on more physical pursuits. She had a particular fondness for horses and took every opportunity to ride them. She became an expert rider at an early age and especially enjoyed mounting stubborn and unbroken horses. The more difficult they were, the more determined she was to break them. That perseverance proved to be a valuable character trait when, in 1865, her parents gave up their efforts at farming, packed their children into a covered wagon, and began the long journey west toward Virginia City, Montana.

Marthy was 13 years old when the trip began. Already, she preferred the company of men to that of her mother or her three little sisters—and she did her best to fit in with them as well. While proper girls wore bonnets and long skirts, Marthy borrowed a pair of her brother's trousers and a buckskin cap. While most girls who would even dare to ride horseback rode sidesaddle, Marthy rode astride like her father and brothers. And while her sisters stayed with the women to help cook and clean, Marthy chose to ride ahead and hunt with the men in the party. Her participation earned her the respect of many men on the journey and helped her develop considerable skills with a rifle. "By the time we reached Virginia City, I was

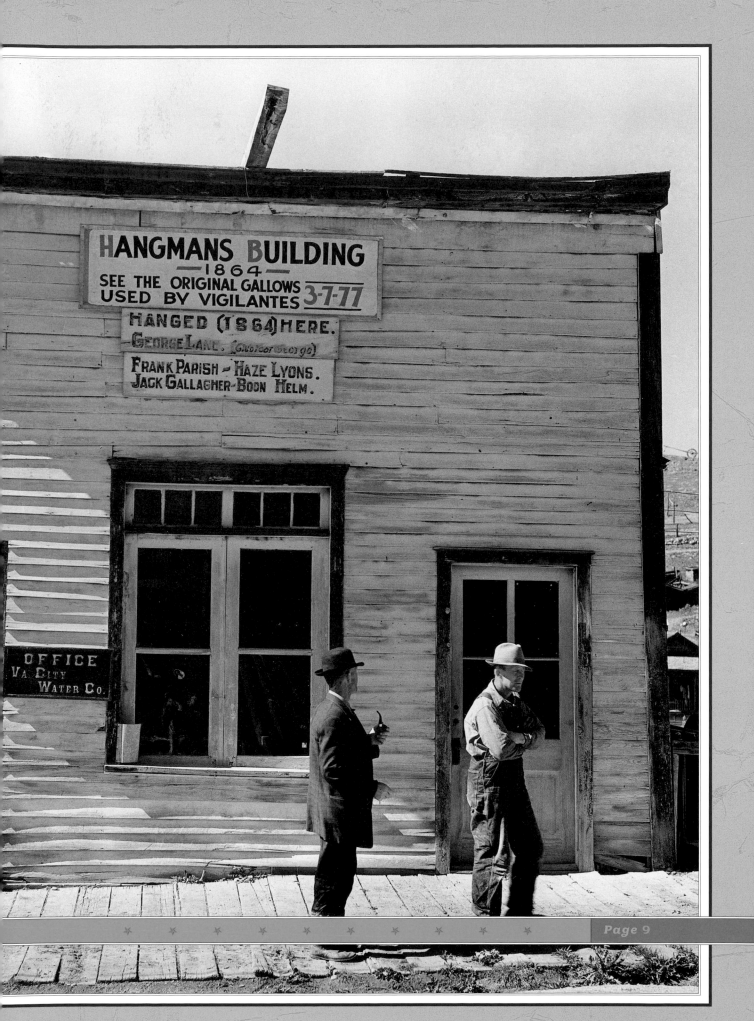

In 1865, Martha Jane Cannary's parents uprooted the family from Missouri and headed west, to Virginia City, Montana (pictured, 1930s).

George Armstrong Custer

By the time General George Armstrong Custer headed west for the Indian wars, he was already a respected leader known for his courage fighting in the Civil War. His cavalry units, in fact, played a critical role in forcing the retreat of renowned Confederate general Robert E. Lee. But it is the story of his own defeat that is far better known. On June 25, 1876, General Custer and the Seventh Cavalry surrounded the Little Bighorn River in eastern Montana. He thought their number, more than 200 strong, would easily be able to overwhelm the Lakota Indians encamped there. He was wrong. The Battle of the Little Bighorn, otherwise known as Custer's Last Stand, was a devastating defeat for the U.S. Army. Custer and all of his men were killed that day. Most of the men were buried where they lay; Custer, however, was later reburied at West Point, New York, with full military honors.

considered a remarkable good shot and a fearless rider for a girl of my age," she remembered in her autobiography.

The route from Princeton, situated in the far northern part of Missouri, to Virginia City, in the Rocky Mountains of eastern Montana, was long and rough. The travelers had to cross rugged, mostly unsettled terrain. They had to climb mountains, cross rivers, and ford streams. When the trail got too steep and rough for the horses, the party had to lower the wagons over ledges by hand with ropes. When torrential rains caused streams and rivers to overflow their banks, the travelers had to carefully scout out safe places to cross. Quicksand and bogs were constant threats to both people and horses.

It was all a great adventure for Martha Jane. "I was at all times with the men when there was excitement and adventures to be had," she wrote in her autobiography. She started picking up the coarse language of the men and even developed a taste for whiskey during the trip. She never missed an opportunity to flirt with danger. While the others looked for safe river crossings, for example, she led her pony into the water and attempted to swim across on her own "merely to amuse myself," she wrote. "I had many narrow escapes from having both myself and pony washed away to certain death."

Marthy and the rest of her family did make it safely to Virginia City after five months. But they did not stay rooted there for long. The Cannarys were farmers, and the land in

With her gun-shooting, tobacco-chewing ways, Martha Jane often mimicked the style of dress of the men of her day quite convincingly.

Virginia City was rough, dry, and rocky. Located just north and west of what is now Yellowstone National Park, the city was far from decent farmland. Gold discovered in a nearby creek likely drew the Cannary family to the area, but by the time they arrived, more than 15,000 gold diggers were already there. The settlement was crowded with prospectors, and there was little housing left for newcomers. Martha Jane and her family probably slept under their wagons or in crudely built shelters during their brief stay. Before long, they had taken to the trail again, heading farther west.

By 1866, they reached Black Foot, Montana. But then the story turns sour. Charlotte Cannary, who sometimes took in laundry from mining camps to help earn extra money, died of "washtub pneumonia" early that year. After burying her, the rest of the family mournfully turned south and went into Utah, settling in Salt Lake City. Again, tragedy struck: Robert Cannary, Marthy's father, died there in 1867. At the age of 15, Martha Jane Cannary was on her own.

Marthy and her siblings did not stay together for long after their father died. No one knows what became of the other five. Martha Jane wandered the West on her own. She worked as a cook or did laundry to support herself. She may have waited tables and tended bar at restaurants or saloons. But such domestic chores were far too tame for a wild woman like Martha Jane.

Dressed in the buckskin pants and jacket that she had become so comfortable in, Marthy looked an awful lot like a boy. She was tall and thin and had always been athletic and muscular. Although some descriptions from that time call her "attractive" and a "pretty, dark-eyed girl," she could certainly have been mistaken for a strong young man. And indeed she was, because in 1868, she joined a crew of men working on the Union Pacific Railroad near Piedmont, Wyoming.

Her stint with the railway was short-lived, however, due in large part to her flirtatious nature. As soon as her deception was discovered (she was caught skinny-dipping with her pals from work), the crew leader ordered her to leave with the next wagon train east. But Martha Jane Cannary would not go far.

Happy Birthday

Even the exact date of Martha Jane Cannary's birthday is hard to verify. Although she sets the date as May 1, 1852, in her autobiography, *Life and Adventures of Calamity Jane: By Herself*, census records from Mercer County, Ohio, where she was reportedly born, can't confirm that most basic fact. The only listing that comes close is for a farmer named J. T. Canary, originally from Ohio, who was the head of a family of five girls and three boys. Only one of the birth dates comes close to the one Martha Jane claimed—and it belonged to one of the sons. Because there's no real reason not to believe her, and because the exact date may actually be of little consequence, most historians have accepted May 1, 1852, as Calamity Jane's birthday. But some still prefer to follow any mention of that date with a parenthetical disclaimer or to note its lack of credibility with an asterisk.

CHAPTER TWO

☙ Laying Claim to Calamity ❧

MARTHA JANE CANNARY'S

CHOICE OF CLOTHING AGAIN SERVED HER WELL WHEN SHE SHOWED UP IN

Fort Russell, Wyoming, **LOOKING FOR A JOB WITH THE MILITARY.**

❁ ❁ ❁ ❁

The army needed scouts as it pushed westward, and young Marthy was willing and able to fill the post. She claims in her autobiography that she joined General George Armstrong Custer as a scout in 1870 and, dressed in a soldier's uniform, headed for Arizona with the Indian Campaign.

Sioux and Cheyenne Indians annihilated George Armstrong Custer and his cavalry at the Battle of the Little Bighorn on June 25, 1876.

By then, she was a reckless and fearless rider with a good eye and a sharp shot. She craved adventure and certainly seemed to find it as a scout. "I had a great many adventures with the Indians, for as a scout I had a great many dangerous missions to perform," she wrote. "While I was in many close places, I always succeeded in getting away safely."

In 1871, she had returned to Wyoming and continued to work as a scout for the military. It was during this time that she claimed to have been given her famous nickname.

According to her autobiography, she earned the name while on a military campaign out of Goose Creek, Wyoming, with Captain Egan. She was part of the detail sent out to stop an Indian uprising, a bloody mission that lasted several days and left several men dead. On the way back to their post, the group was ambushed, and Captain Egan was shot. Martha Jane heard the shot, saw the captain reel in his saddle, and immediately galloped back to his side. She got there, she says, "in time to catch him as he was falling." She lifted the wounded captain onto her horse and carried him safely to the fort. When he recovered, she says, he laughingly said, "I name you 'Calamity Jane,' the heroine of the plains."

That story has long been disputed as a tall tale, even by Captain Egan. But no matter how the name was given, Calamity Jane loved it—and did her best to live up to it. She drank as hard or perhaps even harder than most men. She developed an extensive vocabulary of curse words and used them frequently. She continued to dress unconventionally and to hold unconventional jobs.

Wild Bill Hickok

J ames "Wild Bill" Hickok was born in Homer, Illinois, in 1837. But the adventurous young man did not stay there for long. He left home in 1856 and became a stagecoach driver, a military scout, a marshal, and perhaps even a spy. How he actually earned his name is as murky as Calamity Jane's story. The most widely accepted version is that a woman watching him stop a lynching proclaimed, "My God, ain't he wild," an adjective that stuck. But Wild Bill's life of adventure came to an end on August 2, 1876. While seated at a poker game, his back to the saloon door, Wild Bill was shot and killed from behind by Jack McCall, a notorious outlaw who claimed Wild Bill had killed his brother. To this day, the hand Wild Bill was holding at that moment—a pair of eights and a pair of aces—is known as a "dead man's hand."

Timeline 1875   The rush for gold in the Black Hills begins; shortly after, Calamity Jane meets Wild Bill Hickok.

One of those jobs was as a bullwhacker—a driver of four- to six-hitch teams of oxen that pulled heavy wagons laden with goods all over the West. She earned a decent wage (certainly more than most women could make cooking or doing laundry) and was given free meals, too. She also had plenty of opportunities to practice her swearing, as the men she rode with were legendary for their use of profanity. As usual, Calamity Jane became quite good at her job—or so she said. She liked to brag that she got so good with a whip that she could pick a fly off an ox's ear "four times out of five."

In 1875, Calamity Jane claims to have again joined General Custer as a scout. This time she headed into the Black Hills, where gold had been discovered, to protect the miners and settlers from the Indians in the area. Shortly thereafter, she ended up in Fort Laramie, Wyoming, where she met Wild Bill Hickok. In 1876, the two of them made their way to Deadwood, South Dakota.

Named for the dead trees found in the canyon that became the town's main street, Deadwood attracted all sorts of characters. Wild Bill and Calamity Jane fit right in with the rowdy miners and gamblers there. Calamity Jane claimed the two were married in Deadwood and was known to produce a scrap of faded paper allegedly confirming that fact. Wild Bill was already legally married at the time, and although there is no question that the two shared at least a strong friendship, it is unlikely that they ever legally married.

Calamity Jane's attachment to Wild Bill was quite clear after he was shot to death while playing poker at the Number 10 Saloon in Deadwood. Calamity was working as a Pony Express rider, covering a distance of about 50 miles (80 km) between Deadwood and Custer, South Dakota. On August 2, 1876, she returned from one of those trips to find Wild Bill dead.

Calamity Jane vowed to avenge Wild Bill's murder and reportedly did chase down the killer, a notorious outlaw named Jack McCall. Despite her threatening words, however, it was the law that eventually caught up with him. McCall was tried and hanged in Yankton, South Dakota, for the murder of Wild Bill.

Hickok's death deeply affected Calamity Jane, who began to drink even more than usual. Still, when smallpox struck the city, she was a valiant nurse to many of the patients. She was said to have nursed many ill patients back to health and was compared by some to Florence Nightingale, a nursing pioneer who became famous for her efforts during the Crimean War.

But Calamity herself, it seems, preferred to be remembered for her more rough-and-tumble heroics. She liked to tell about how she single-handedly saved a stagecoach and its passengers from hostile Indians just outside of Deadwood. She saw the horses running toward her and noticed that they were being pursued by Indians. So she waited for the coach by the barn, where the horses knew to stop, and came alongside the coach. There she could see that the driver had already been slain.

One of the slickest-looking, quickest draws in the West, Wild Bill Hickok was by some accounts a husband to Calamity Jane.

"When the stage got to the station the Indians hid in the bushes," she wrote in her autobiography. "I immediately removed all the baggage from the coach except the mail. I then took the driver's seat and with all haste drove to Deadwood, carrying the six passengers and the dead driver."

Calamity Jane did not linger long in Deadwood. She briefly joined the cavalry again before leaving the military to prospect on her own. She wandered from the Dakotas to Wyoming to California and ended up in El Paso, Texas, in 1884. There, she met and married Clinton Burk in August 1885. Although she had been linked romantically to many men and had claimed marriage to about a dozen of them, this was her first substantiated marriage. "I thought I had traveled through life long enough alone and thought it was time to take a partner for the rest of my days," she wrote.

Calamity Jane stayed settled long enough to have a baby girl, born on October 28, 1887. The baby was "the very image of its father," Calamity noted in her autobiography, but with "the temper of its mother." But her marriage, like her attempt at motherhood, was not successful. Some say Burk left her; others say that she deserted him. In any case, the two did not stay together. Nor did the baby girl stay with her mother. Although no one knows for sure what happened to the child, some reports place her in the care of nuns at a convent school in South Dakota.

The Battle of the Little Bighorn

Among the many tall tales Calamity Jane told about herself was the story of why she, a scout in General George Armstrong Custer's company, was not at the Battle of the Little Bighorn. She said that in the spring of 1876, she was ordered to swim across the Platte River as the bearer of important dispatches, then ride 90 miles (145 km) soaking wet. In the process, she became seriously ill and had to be hospitalized for 14 days. If she had not been sidelined by that illness, she would most certainly have accompanied General Custer to the Little Bighorn. And of course, she would most certainly have also perished with Custer and his troops, who were slaughtered by a coalition of Indian tribes on June 25, 1876. No one has been able to confirm this version of the story, so most people simply consider it one of Calamity Jane's fanciful tales.

CHAPTER THREE

Drunk and Destitute

CALAMITY JANE WAS ENTERING HER FOURTH DECADE

AS THE 1890S BEGAN,

BUT ALREADY THE ONCE-SPIRITED, RED-HAIRED WOMAN

looked and acted much older.

Her face was wrinkled and drawn, and

HER EYES HAD LOST MUCH OF THEIR SPARK.

Her years of heavy drinking were taking a toll on both her appearance and her health. She neglected to take care of herself and often stumbled from saloon to saloon clad only in rags. Although she was never charged with a crime, she spent many nights in jail, sobering up from a drunken binge.

Still, Calamity Jane continued to roam the West, eventually making her way back to Deadwood, South Dakota. It was October 1895 when she returned, after an absence of more than 15 years. Her arrival, she wrote, "created quite an excitement among my many friends of the past." She said that newcomers to the city were anxious to meet the fabled Calamity Jane and to be regaled with her adventurous tales. She was only too happy to oblige.

Among those who reportedly sat for her adventurous stories were men from the East, who quickly encouraged Calamity Jane to join a Western show and share her tales with the public at large. Buffalo Bill Cody's *Wild West* show was a roaring success, and Calamity Jane seemed a natural fit for such a show. She could tell of her treacherous trek from Missouri to Montana. She could recount her days scouting Indians with the U.S. Army. She could spin tales about Wild Bill Hickok and the uproarious days in Deadwood.

Western shows, such as *Buffalo Bill's Wild West and Congress of Rough Riders of the World*, had become immensely popular throughout the eastern United States and abroad, where people knew nothing about life in the American West. The productions introduced people to the romantic image of the West. Some of it was true, of course, and some was not. The shows included cowboys and Indians, buffalo hunters and army scouts, sharpshooters and stunt riders, and even reenactments of such famous

As this photograph shows, Calamity Jane could look right at home—even intimidating—in buckskin clothes, astride a horse.

Buffalo Bill

Born as William Frederick Cody in Scott County, Iowa, in 1846, Buffalo Bill became most famous for the Wild West show he organized in 1883. But even before he was touring both America and Europe with his troupe of western entertainers, Buffalo Bill was living the life himself. As a boy, he rode for the Pony Express. He served as both a Union scout and a soldier during the Civil War. He earned a reputation as an excellent marksman who provided fresh buffalo meat to hardworking soldiers and railroad workers. After serving as a guide during the Indian wars, he decided to start his own business. *Buffalo Bill's Wild West and Congress of Rough Riders of the World* introduced Americans and Europeans to Western legends such as sharpshooter Annie Oakley and even Chief Sitting Bull. Buffalo Bill died in 1917 at the age of 70. He is buried atop Lookout Mountain near Denver, Colorado.

battles as Custer's Last Stand. Stars such as Annie Oakley and Buffalo Bill had become household names through such shows.

Calamity Jane was happy to give show business a try. She made her first appearance at the Palace Museum in Minneapolis, Minnesota, on January 20, 1896. For a dime, viewers could listen to her tell about all of her Western exploits. She was billed as the "famous woman scout of the Wild West" and "the heroine of a thousand thrilling adventures." Advertisements called her "the terror of evildoers in the Black Hills" and "the comrade of Buffalo Bill and Wild Bill Hickok."

But Calamity Jane was not a natural performer. She seemed overly self-conscious and stiff onstage. She was tongue-tied and embarrassed and seemed to dislike having an audience staring at her. Her first instinct, unfortunately, was to turn back to alcohol after having made a promise to stop drinking. Alcohol may have given her more courage, but it did nothing for her stage presence. After appearing for a few too many performances in a sadly drunken state, Calamity Jane was fired from the show.

She tried to find work with other shows and was said to have traveled for a time with *Buffalo Bill's Wild West*, but the same problems always forced her out. Then, in the late 1890s, someone helped her write a short memoir of her life. She called it *Life and Adventures of Calamity Jane: By Herself* and signed it

In a final, failed adventure, Calamity Jane took her memoirs to the Pan-American Exhibition in Buffalo, New York (pictured).

"Mrs. M. Burk, better known as Calamity Jane."

When the booklet was printed, Calamity Jane agreed to take it to the 1901 Pan-American Exposition in Buffalo, New York, and try to sell it. She eagerly went east for a new adventure. But this one would not go as well as she had hoped.

The Exposition, a much-anticipated fair designed to spotlight all of the latest technology as well as to entertain the masses, attracted eight million people. People came to see the spectacular Electric Tower, which was illuminated nightly by thousands of colored bulbs and floodlights. They came to try out the entertainment in the midway. They came to participate in athletic competitions and musical events. In the process, they also got to see one of the most notorious women of the West, Calamity Jane.

But once again, Calamity Jane didn't handle the attention well. The experience was so humiliating that she again began to drink, which landed her in trouble with the local police. Some say that she had to ask her old friend Buffalo Bill for a loan to help her get home. However she managed to do it, she fled back to the West as fast as she could.

Even back in familiar territory, Calamity Jane could not find her way back to glory. Her years of hard living had caught up with her. She was broke, in poor health, and alone. She continued to drink, but most of her adventurous spirit was gone. People who saw her were astonished by her appearance. One storekeeper in Wyoming recalled a "nondescript woman who had the appearance of great age" drifting into town and could hardly believe it was the legendary Calamity Jane. "All traces of her former vitality and aggressiveness were gone," he said. "She . . . looked 80."

It was 1903, and she was only 51.

That summer, a broke and desperate Calamity Jane made her way back to Deadwood one last time. On August 1, 1903, a few weeks after she arrived in the area, she died of pneumonia in a small rented room in the Calloway Hotel in Terry, South Dakota.

Calamity Jane had long requested that she be buried in Deadwood, near her old friend Wild Bill Hickok. Despite all of her drinking and carrying on, the people of Deadwood recognized her contributions to their city and respected her wishes. The Old Pioneer Society of Deadwood put together a proper funeral for Calamity, even dressing her in a grand white dress instead of the men's clothing or stark black dresses she preferred.

After the funeral, said to be one of the largest ever held for a woman in Deadwood, her flower-covered coffin was carried to the Mount Moriah Cemetery, on a hill overlooking the city. Calamity Jane was laid to rest there, beside Wild Bill.

Wild Bill's Baby

No one has been able to substantiate claims that Calamity Jane and Wild Bill were married, much less that she gave birth to his baby. Still, almost a quarter-century after Calamity Jane's death, a woman came forward claiming to be their daughter. She said that she had found the story of her birth in her mother's diary in an old trunk. According to the story, Calamity Jane gave birth to a baby girl in a cave near Deadwood not long after Wild Bill was murdered. The two were discovered there by a captain with the famous Cunard steamship line who was happily married but without children. He agreed to adopt the baby girl and to give her the life Calamity Jane knew she couldn't provide. The only problem was that the name given to the captain in the story—Captain O'Neil—didn't match any employment records for the Cunard line. And, after an initial flurry of attention, the woman claiming to be Calamity Jane's daughter disappeared from the spotlight. No other verification has ever been offered.

CHAPTER FOUR

The Legend Grows

THE LEGEND OF CALAMITY JANE HAS GROWN IN THE CENTURY

SINCE HER DEATH,

DUE IN LARGE PART TO HER OWN STORYTELLING.

Like many of the prominent characters of that era,

SHE ENJOYED EMBELLISHING THE DETAILS OF HER LIFE—

more as a form of entertainment than anything else. But as historians have compared accounts and records from the time in which Calamity Jane lived, they've been able to find few hard and fast facts.

What they do know is this: Calamity Jane indeed lived a wild and adventurous life, and certainly did many daring and reckless acts. She can be placed in Deadwood at roughly the same time as Wild Bill, although what she did there is not entirely clear. No one knows if she ever learned to read or write, or if she attended school at all.

Calamity Jane (in rare dress, left) was never one to refuse a drink with the boys, as she shows in this photograph taken in Montana.

It's quite clear that not all of the stories Calamity Jane told about herself are true, and many are likely pure fabrication. But to many people, the distinction between fact and fiction doesn't matter. More important is the legend that has grown up around Calamity Jane and that continues still today.

The romanticized version of her down-and-dirty life actually began while Calamity Jane was still alive. A writer named Edward Lytton Wheeler started using a character named "Calamity Jane" in his novels sometime around 1877. The heroine in Wheeler's *Deadwood Dick* (the title character was likely modeled after Wild Bill) series shared her nerve and sense of adventure with the real Calamity Jane, but perhaps little else. Wheeler's Jane was "regally beautiful" and wore elegant outfits of buckskin and velvet, but Calamity Jane herself was never described in those terms. Most accounts of her life fail to mention her appearance entirely, except to say that she often dressed in ill-fitting men's clothing or in drab black dresses.

Still, Wheeler's dime novels, named for their cost, made Calamity Jane and her legendary life immensely popular. Between 1877 and 1885, he wrote as many as 35 *Deadwood Dick* stories, many of which included Calamity Jane. The tales he told no doubt helped solidify the image of an already notorious woman and probably added to Calamity Jane's own repertoire as well.

Edward Lytton Wheeler

Very little is known about novelist Edward Lytton Wheeler. His characters, especially Deadwood Dick and Calamity Jane, are far better known than he is. But the New York-born novelist played an important role in sustaining the legend of Calamity Jane. Wheeler was probably just 20 years old when he started writing, first for the popular story papers and the *Saturday Journal*. Before long, however, he was writing short "novelettes," many of which were published as part of the *Ten Cent Pocket Library*. In 1877, he penned the first episode of his famous *Deadwood Dick* adventures. Wheeler tried to extend his earning power by managing a theatrical company, too, most likely to put on his own play, *Deadwood Dick, a Road Agent. A Drama of the Gold Mines*. That venture was notably unsuccessful. Wheeler continued writing dime novels for the balance of his life (he is believed to have died in 1885 or 1886) but never became more popular than the heroes he created.

It was years after her death in 1903 that stories about Calamity Jane began to circulate in earnest again, spurred partly by a tabloid-style tribute titled *Calamity Jane and the Lady Wildcats*, which romanticized her exploits and exaggerated her acts of courage. By then, it was the 1920s, and women were beginning to cut their hair short and break out of stereotypical roles. The "flappers" of the time were notorious for many of the same behaviors that Calamity Jane enjoyed: drinking, using harsh language, socializing with men, and wearing unconventional clothes. One popular writer of the time summed up the renewed appeal of Calamity Jane by saying, "She swore, she drank, she wore men's clothing. She was just ahead of her time."

The legend of Calamity Jane has had a timeless appeal. Dozens of books, both fiction and nonfiction, have been written about her life. Some are scholarly attempts to sort out fact from fiction and to unveil the real Calamity Jane. Others are more fanciful looks at her life as a legend. Her name is mentioned in most anthologies about the legends of the West, where she often is included with the "bad guys," even though she was never arrested or charged with a crime.

Filmmakers and playwrights have tackled her story as well. In 1953, Doris Day was cast as the reckless Westerner in the Hollywood movie *Calamity Jane*—and proceeded to portray her more as a genial tomboy than a drunken wanderer.

Several plays have been written about Calamity Jane's life, many of which continue to be produced by small theater companies today. Her character pops up often in movies and other productions about other legends of the West. Even TV producers have been eager to incorporate her character into shows and movies. Most recently, Calamity Jane was portrayed in HBO's original series *Deadwood*, which first aired in 2004, as a harsh, burly woman who was fiercely loyal both to her friends (namely, Wild Bill) and to her bottle.

While Hollywood has had fun portraying the legend of Calamity Jane, thousands of people have had fun exploring her old stomping grounds in Deadwood, South Dakota. The city, which had faded from glory as the gold was wiped out of its hills, was designated as a National Historic Landmark in 1961. In 1989, it became the third place in the United States to legalize gambling. Soon, the historic city was restored to its original beauty, from the brick-paved streets to the stately Victorian mansions along Main Street. It has since become a popular destination for tourists who come to visit the graves of Wild Bill and Calamity Jane and to tour the places they frequented, including the Number 10 Saloon, where reenactments of Wild Bill's murder and the trial of his murderer draw crowds year-round. The city honors Calamity Jane's legacy in many of its publications and promotions, including an art contest soliciting images of Wild Bill and Calamity Jane.

Wild Bill, starring Jeff Bridges as Wild Bill Hickok and Ellen Barkin (pictured) as Calamity Jane, hit American theaters in 1995.

Historians have made some progress in deciphering what is real and what isn't about Calamity Jane's life. The truth, they say, is not as romantic or glorious as some would suggest. Calamity Jane was likely more of a lowlife than a heroic figure. She faced great obstacles on her journey through life but also made her share of bad decisions along the way. She was no doubt a slave to alcohol, and no doubt took some dubious jobs in order to secure her drink of choice. Her outrageous behavior and tall tales certainly alienated many friends and acquaintances, but her death was nonetheless mourned by the people who knew her.

Few people are eager to rewrite the history of the West or of the legends who lived there—including Calamity Jane. Although purists will continue to search for the truth about her life, many others are willing to accept the stories for what they are: the larger-than-life legend of one of the West's wildest women.

Christened as Calamity

Calamity Jane's own wild tale about being christened with her nickname by Captain Egan, whom she saved from hostile Indians, is likely just that. Captain Egan even disputed it himself—and historians have long taken his side. It's not unlikely, however, that someone did bestow the name on her. It was, after all, quite an appropriate adjective for such a precocious young woman. Historians believe that in the Old West, women and girls were commonly referred to as "janes." William Clark, of the Lewis and Clark expedition, even referred to Sacagawea as "Janey" in his journals. So it's not much of a stretch to think that somewhere along the line, someone fittingly added "calamity" to Martha Jane's "jane." However it came to be, the name stuck and was apparently appreciated by its beholder. One report says that whenever she arrived in a new town, she would enter the nearest saloon and announce, "The name's Calamity Jane, and the drinks are on me!"

Further Information

BOOKS

Burk, Martha Jane. *Life and Adventures of Calamity Jane, By Herself.*
N.p.: Ye Galleon Press, 1979.

Calvert, Patricia. *Great Lives: The American Frontier*. New York:
Atheneum Books for Young Readers, 1997.

Green, Carl R., and William R. Sanford. *Calamity Jane: Frontier Original*.
Berkeley Heights, N.J.: Enslow Publishers, 1996.

FILMS

Calamity Jane. 1953. 101 min. Warner Home Video.

Calamity Jane. 1984. 97 min. Twentieth Century Fox.

Wild Women—Calamity Jane, Belle Star, and Annie Oakley. 2001.
50 min. A&E Entertainment.

WEB SITES

About.com: Calamity Jane
http://womenshistory.about.com/library/bio/blbio_calamity_jane.htm

Deadwood.org
http://www.deadwood.org

Encyclopedia Britannica: Women in American History
http://www.search.eb.com/women/articles/Calamity_Jane.html

Index